I0476635

Creative Mandalas 3

Mandala Coloring Books Vol.3

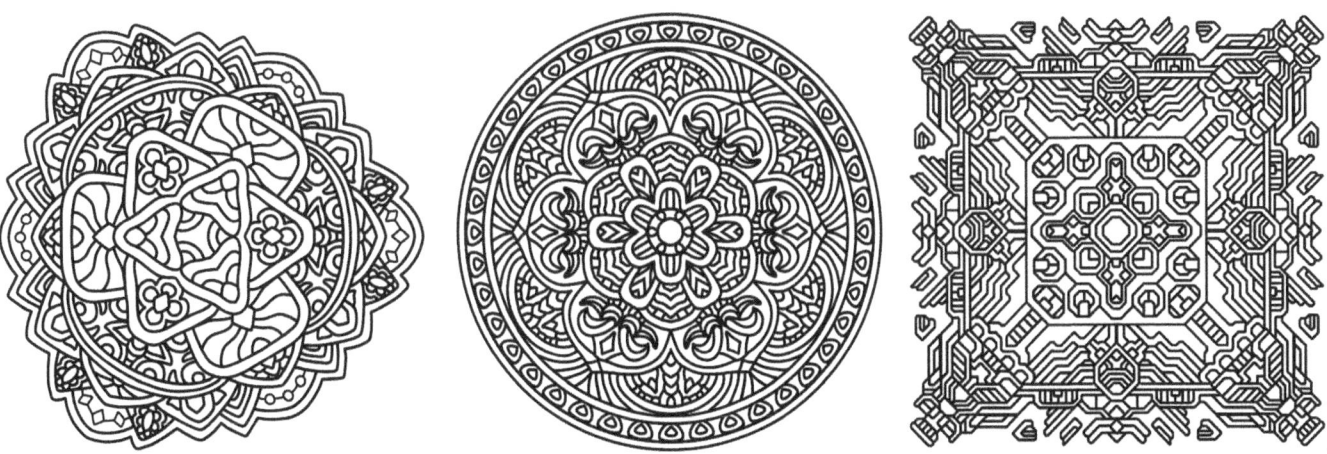

Karim Benyagoub

Copyright © 2015 Karim Benyagoub

All rights reserved

ISBN-10: 1514181002

ISBN-13: 978-1514181003

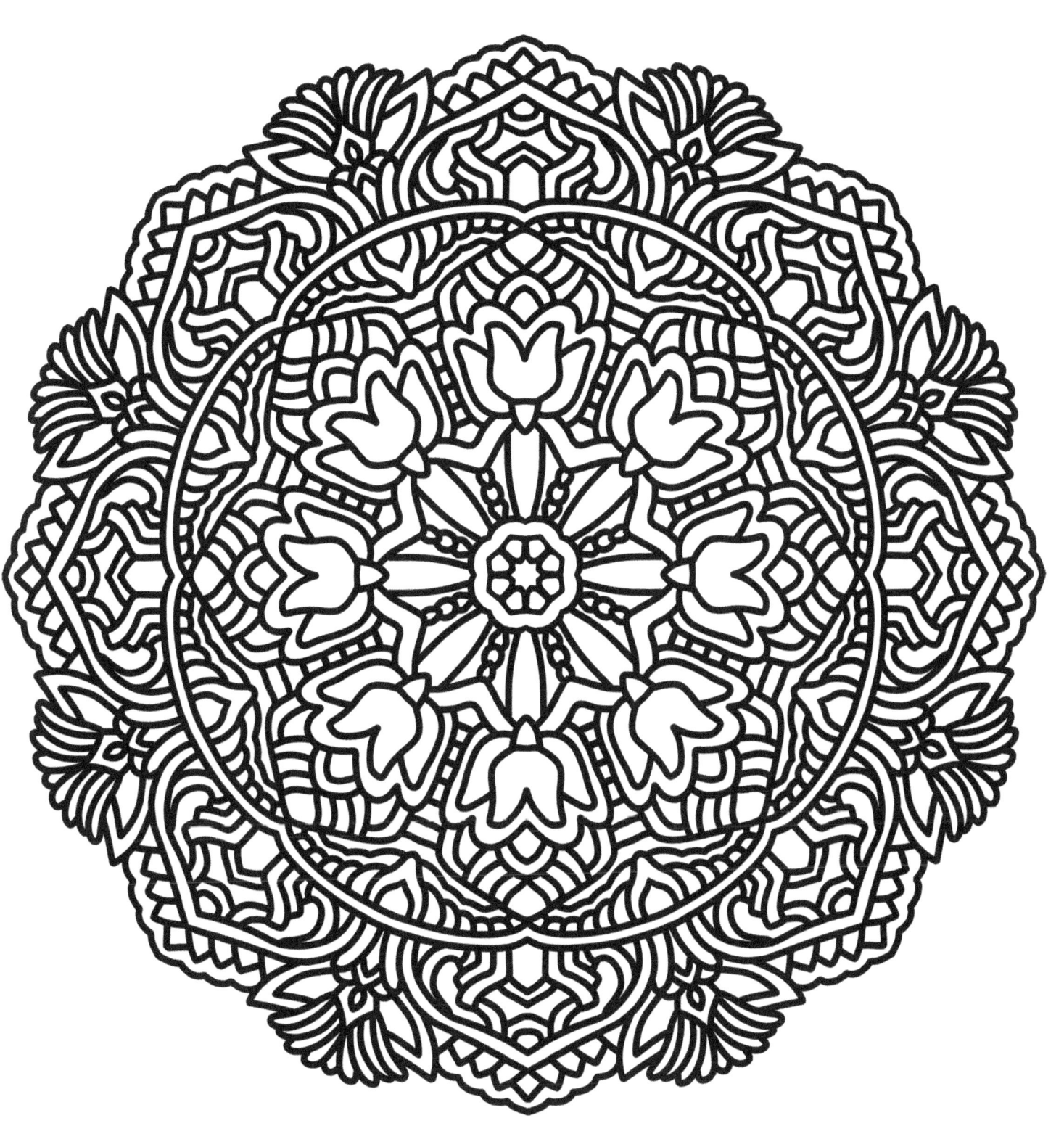

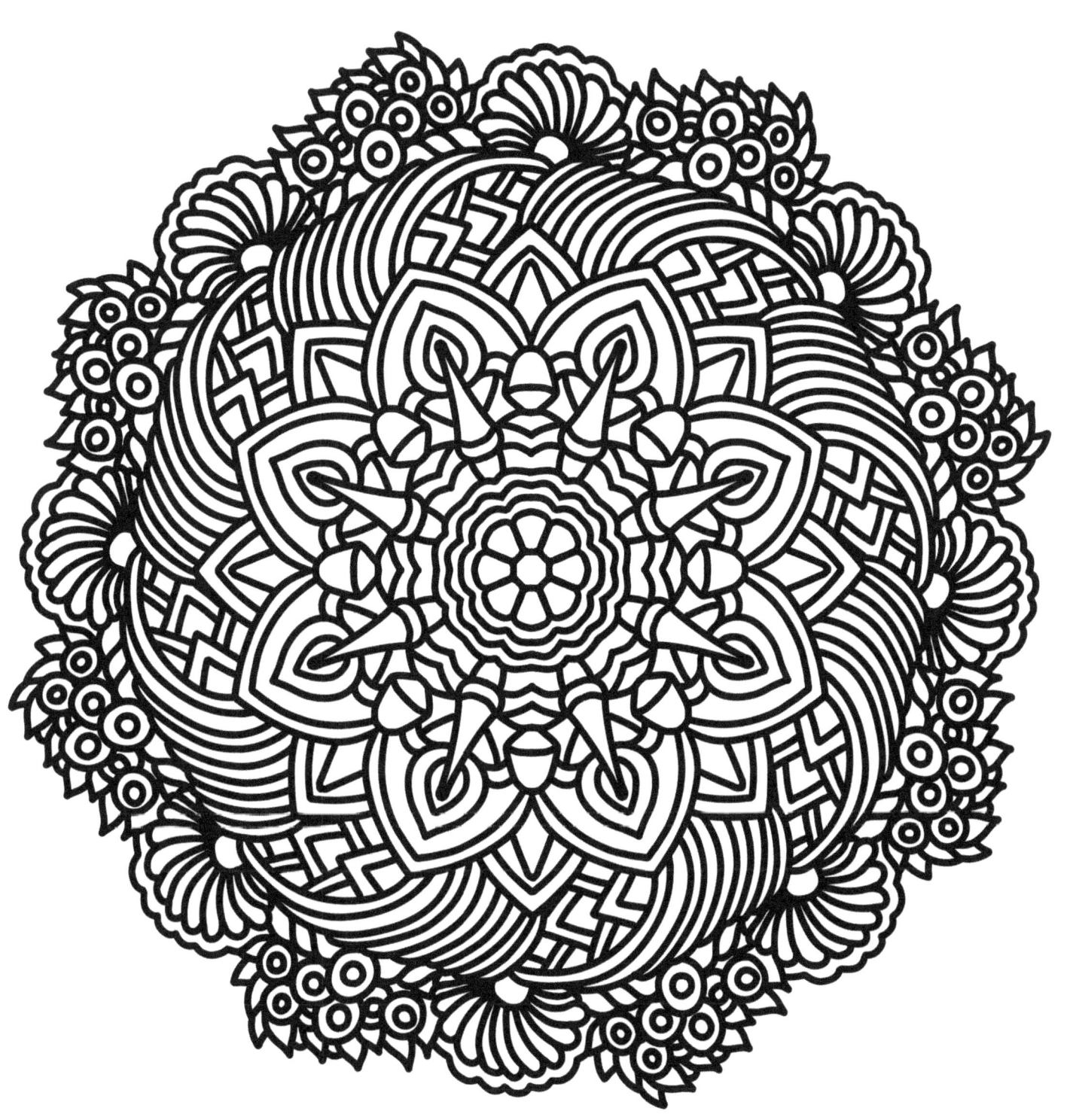

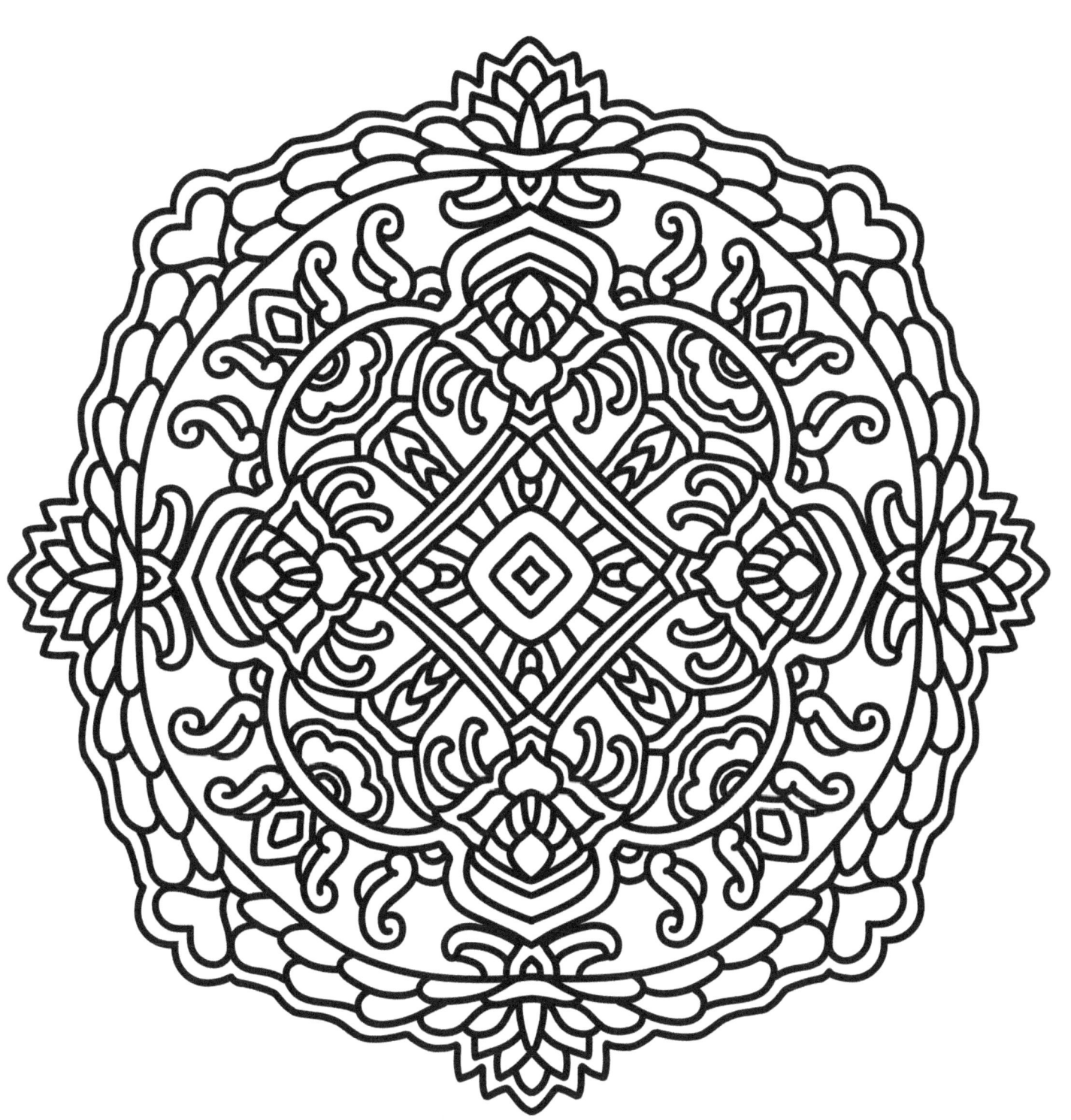

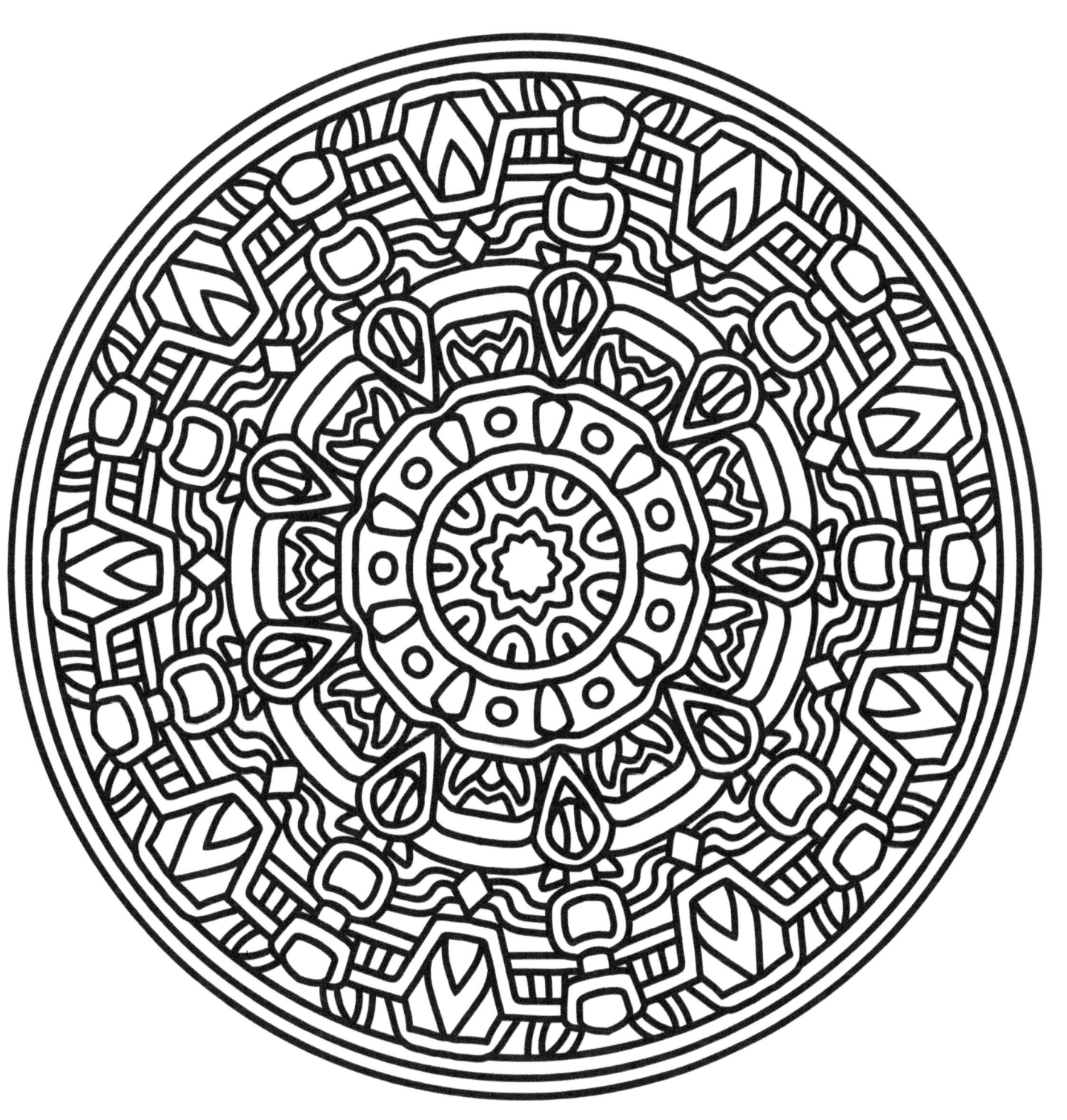

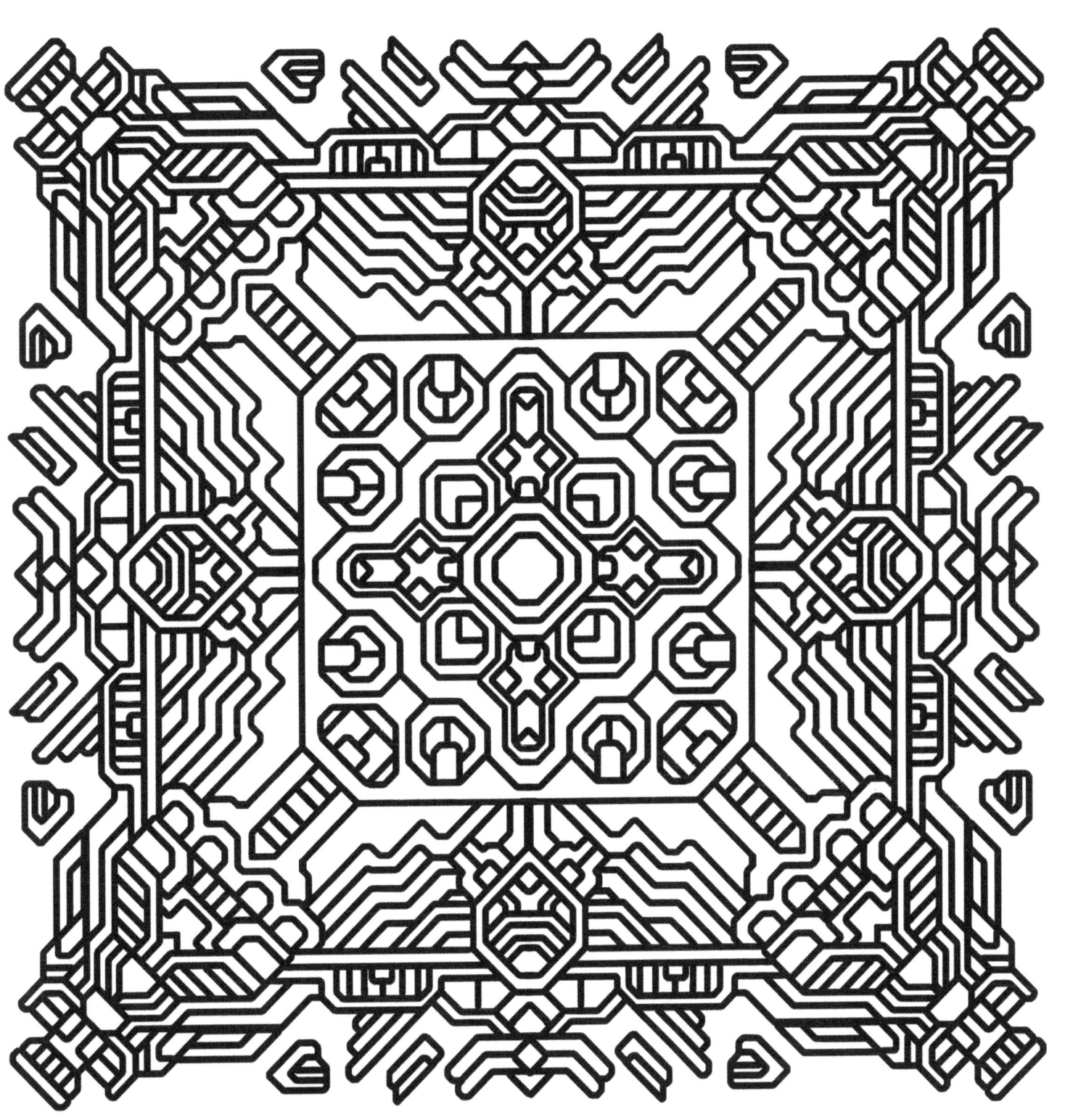

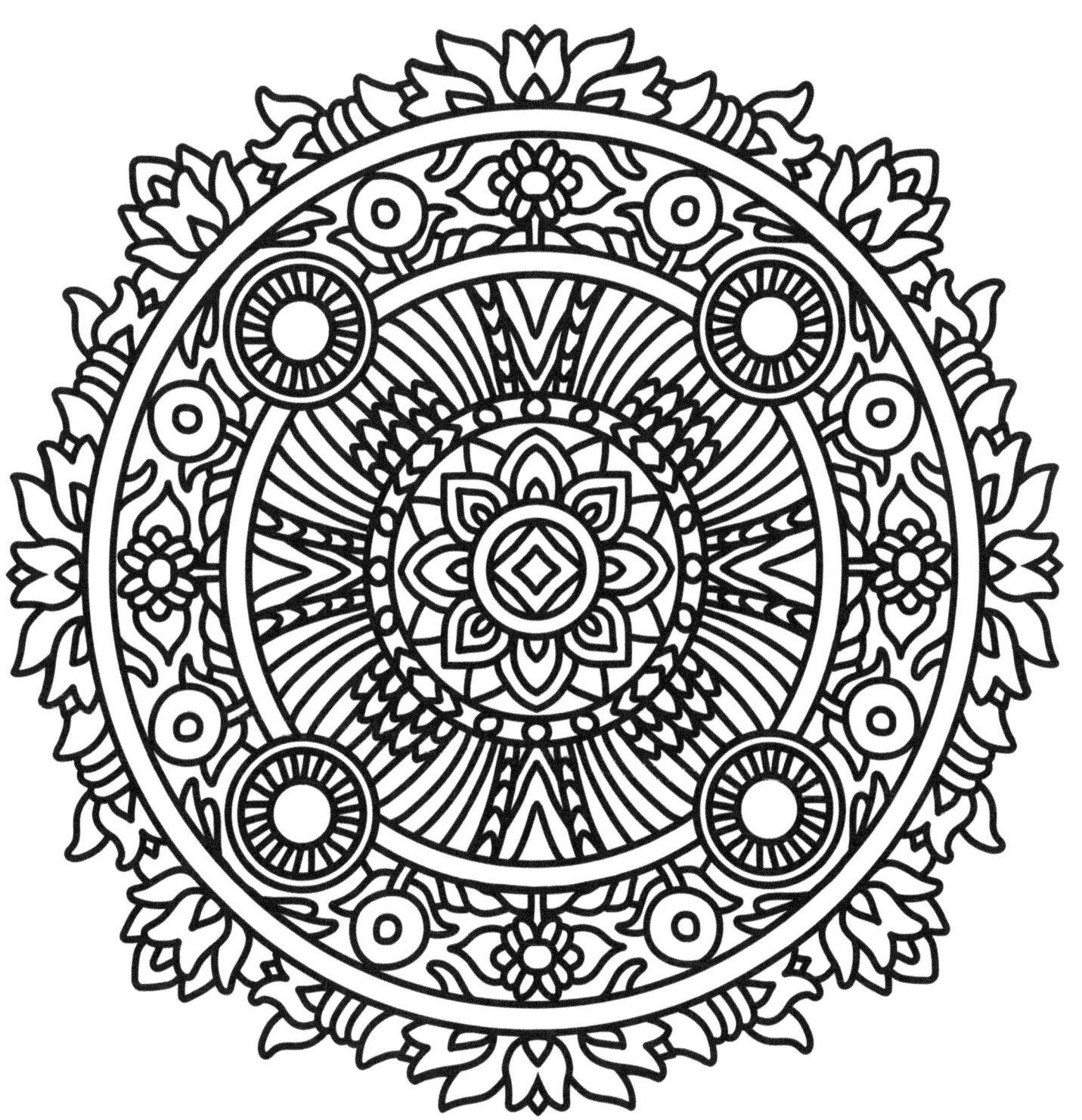

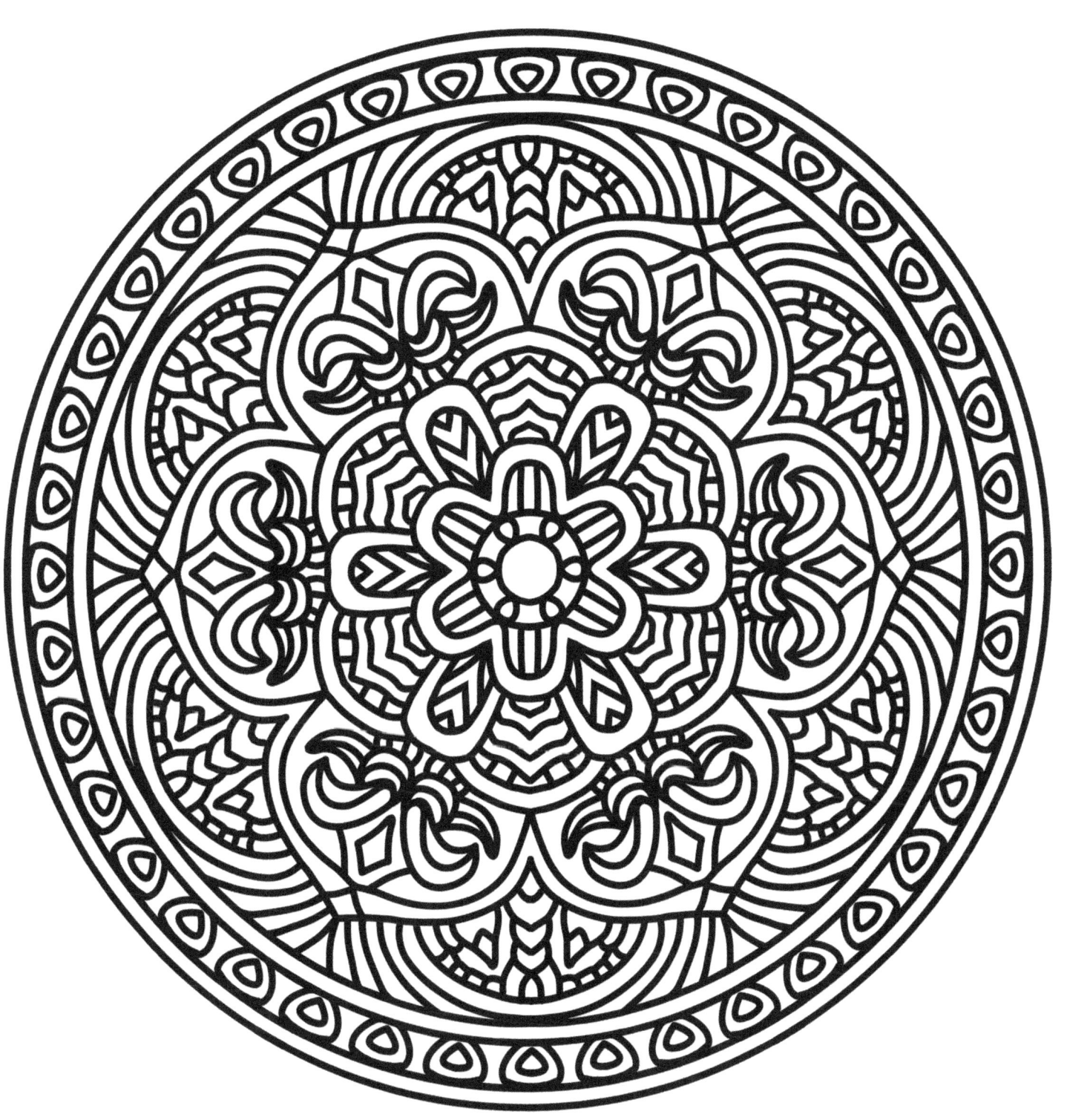

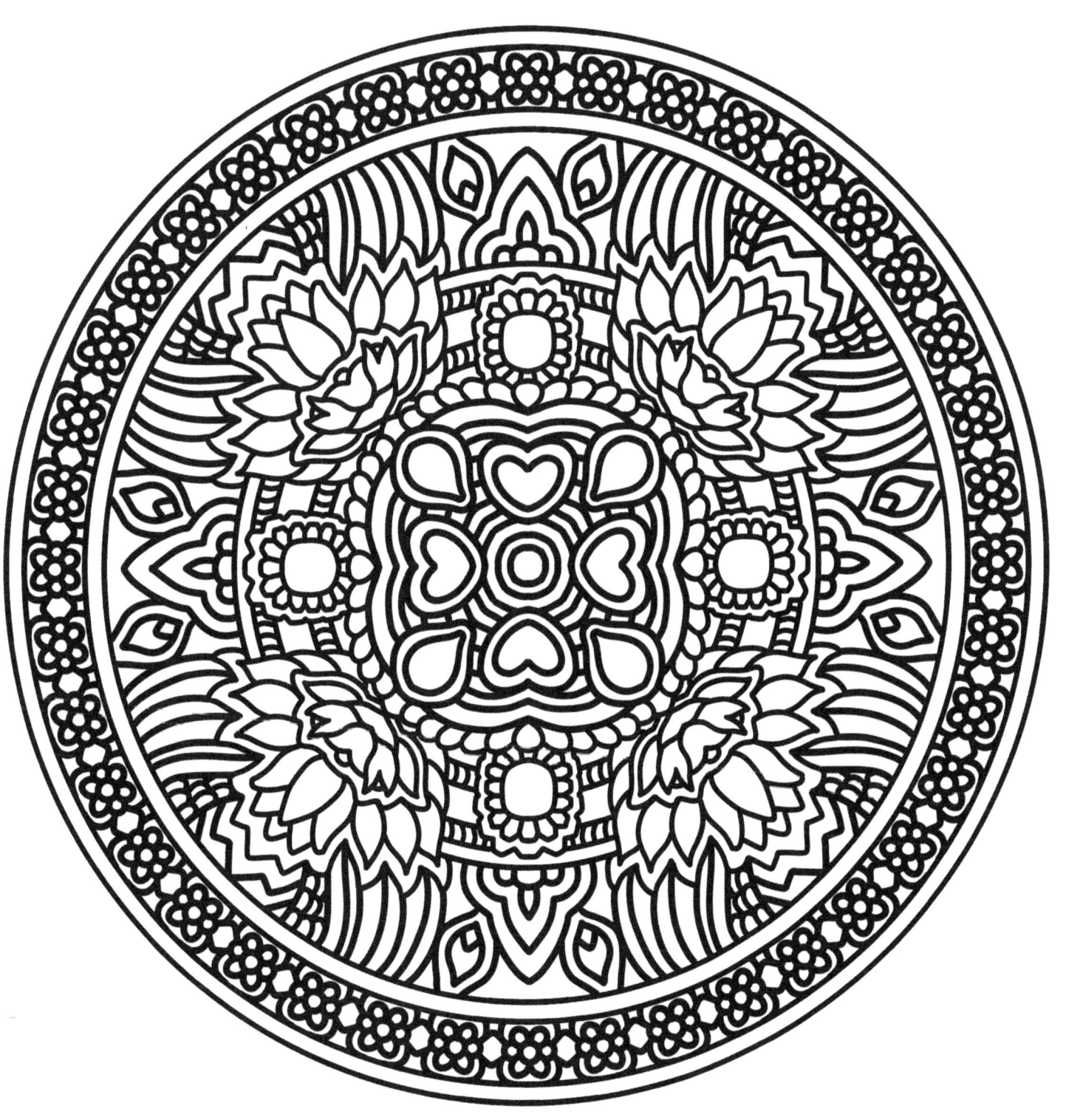

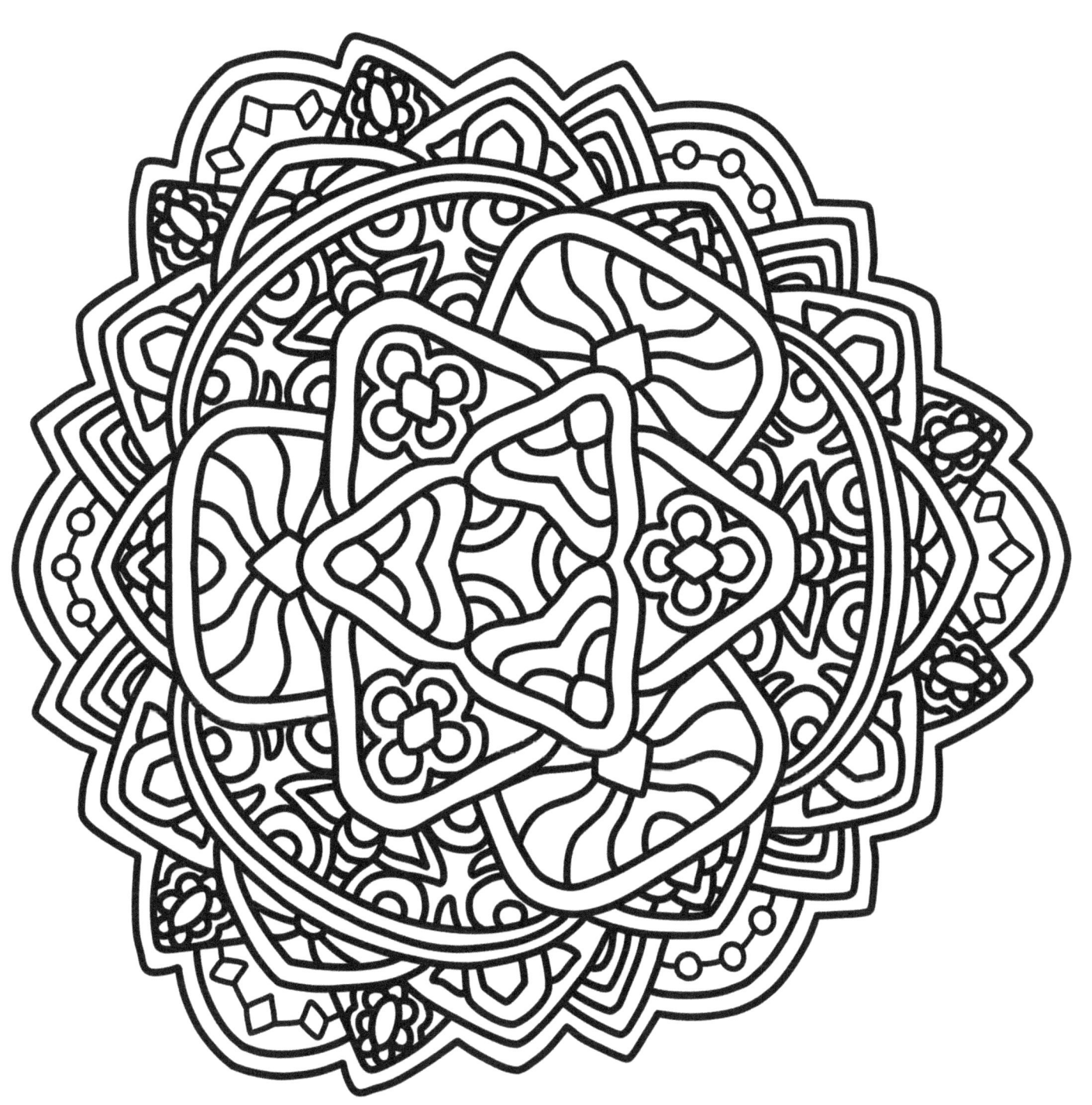

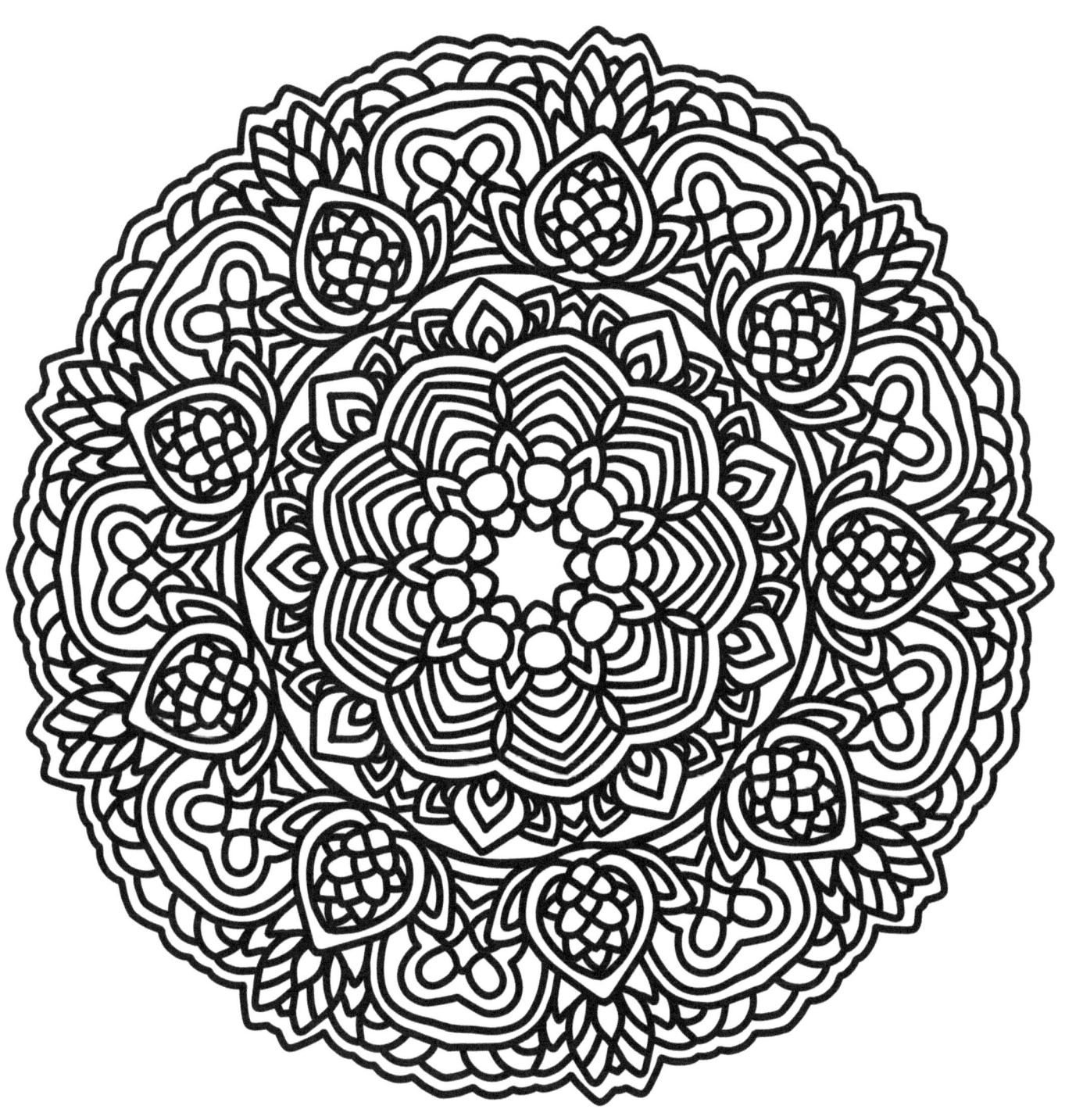

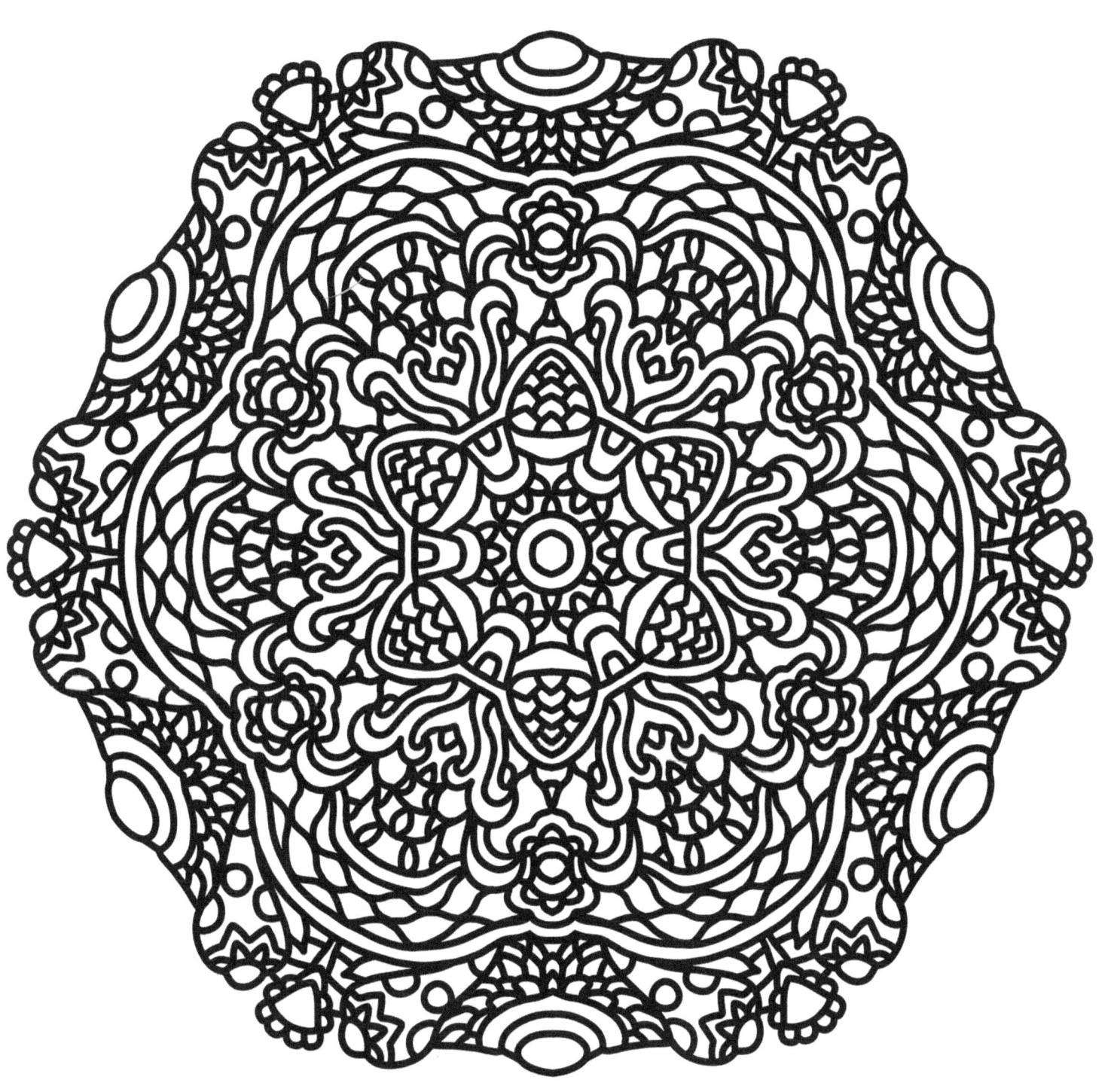

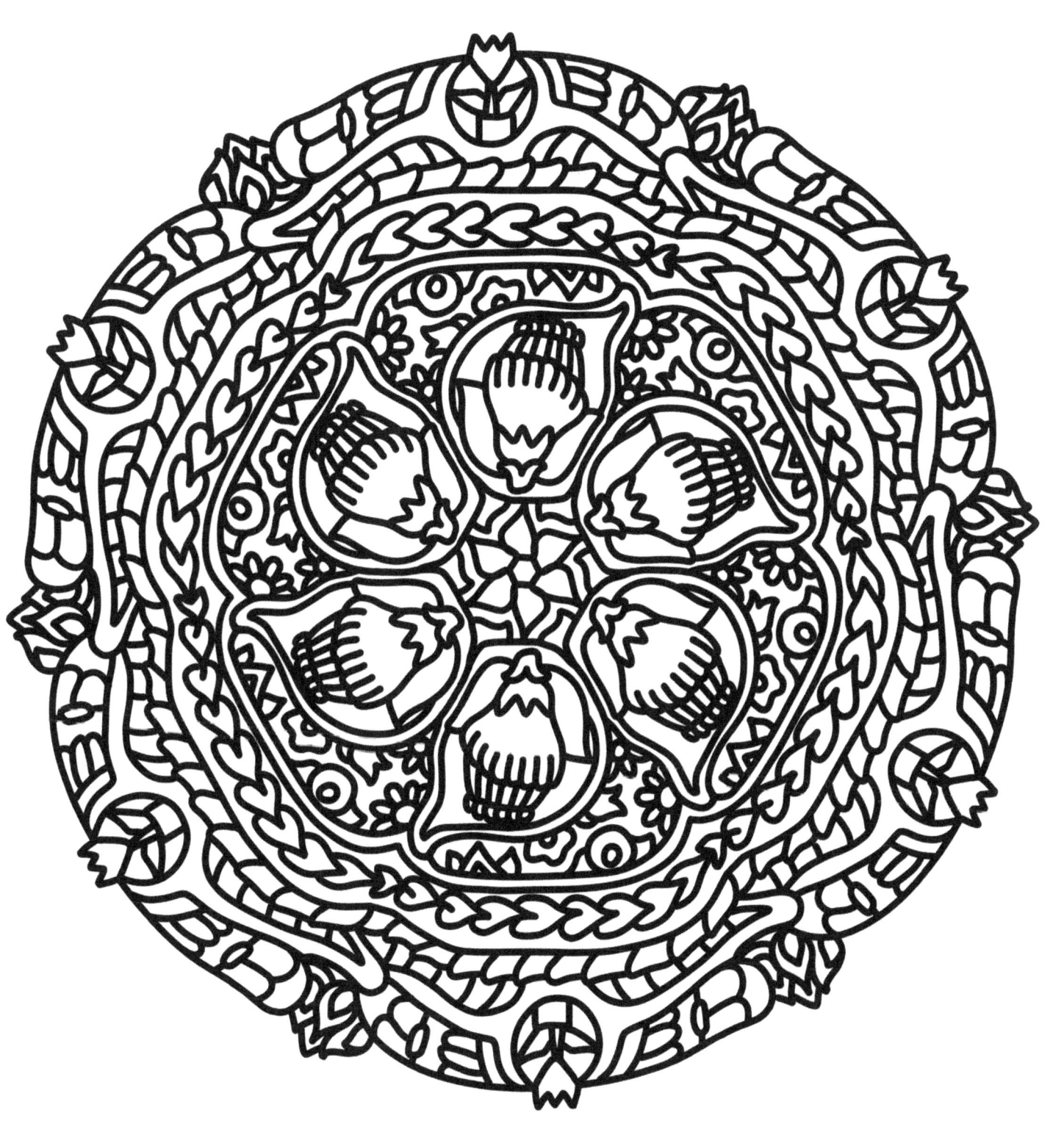

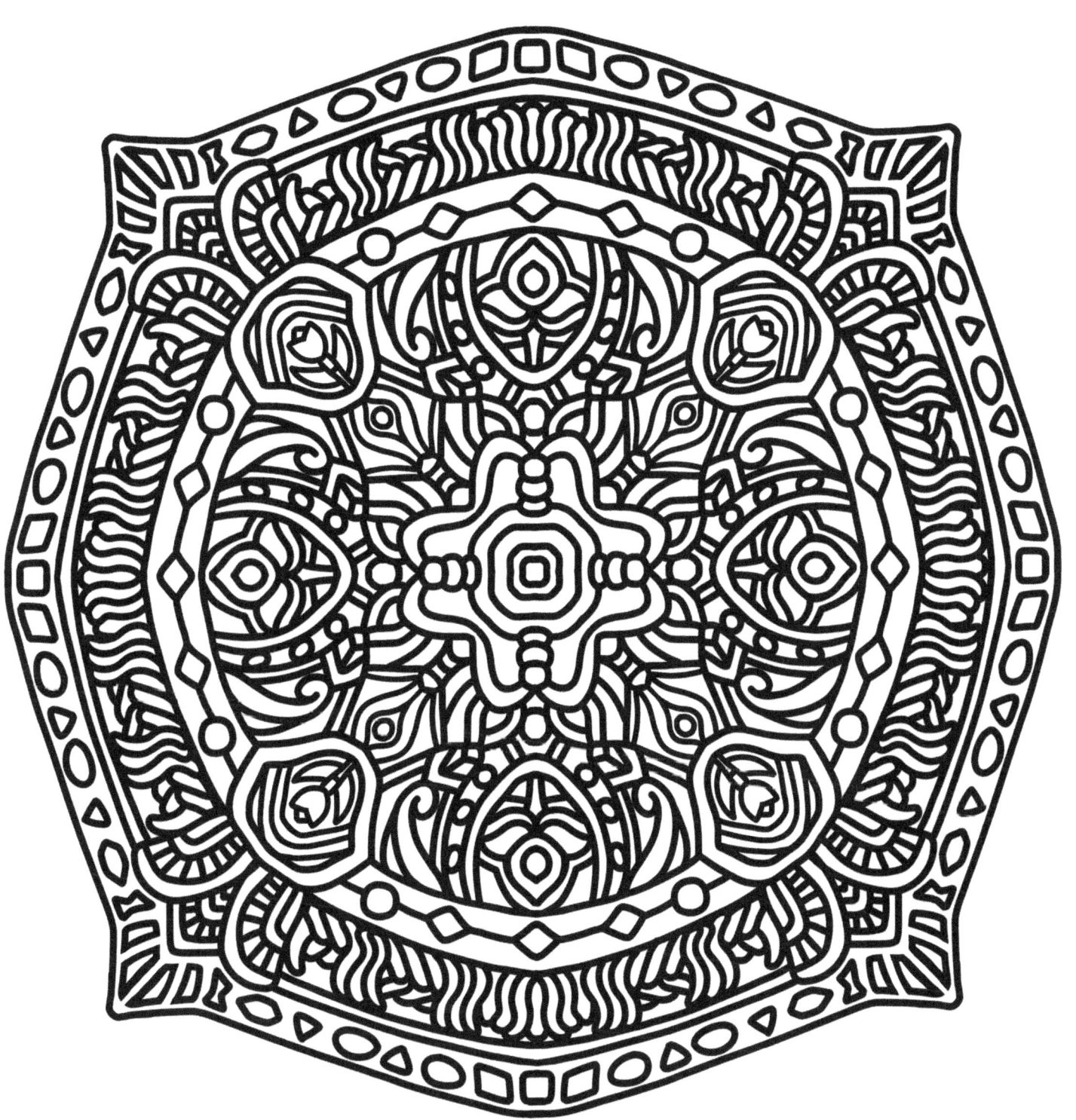

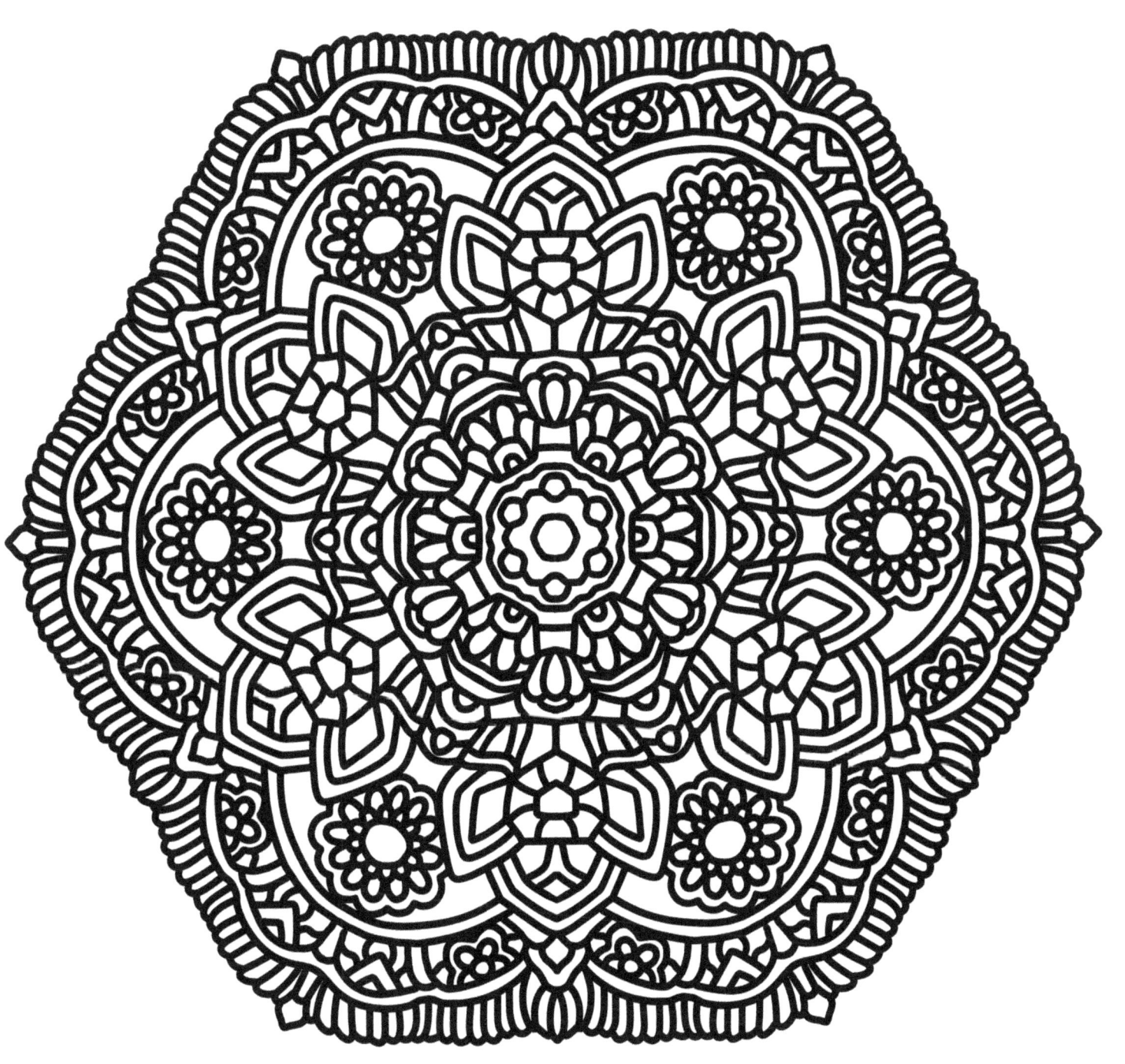

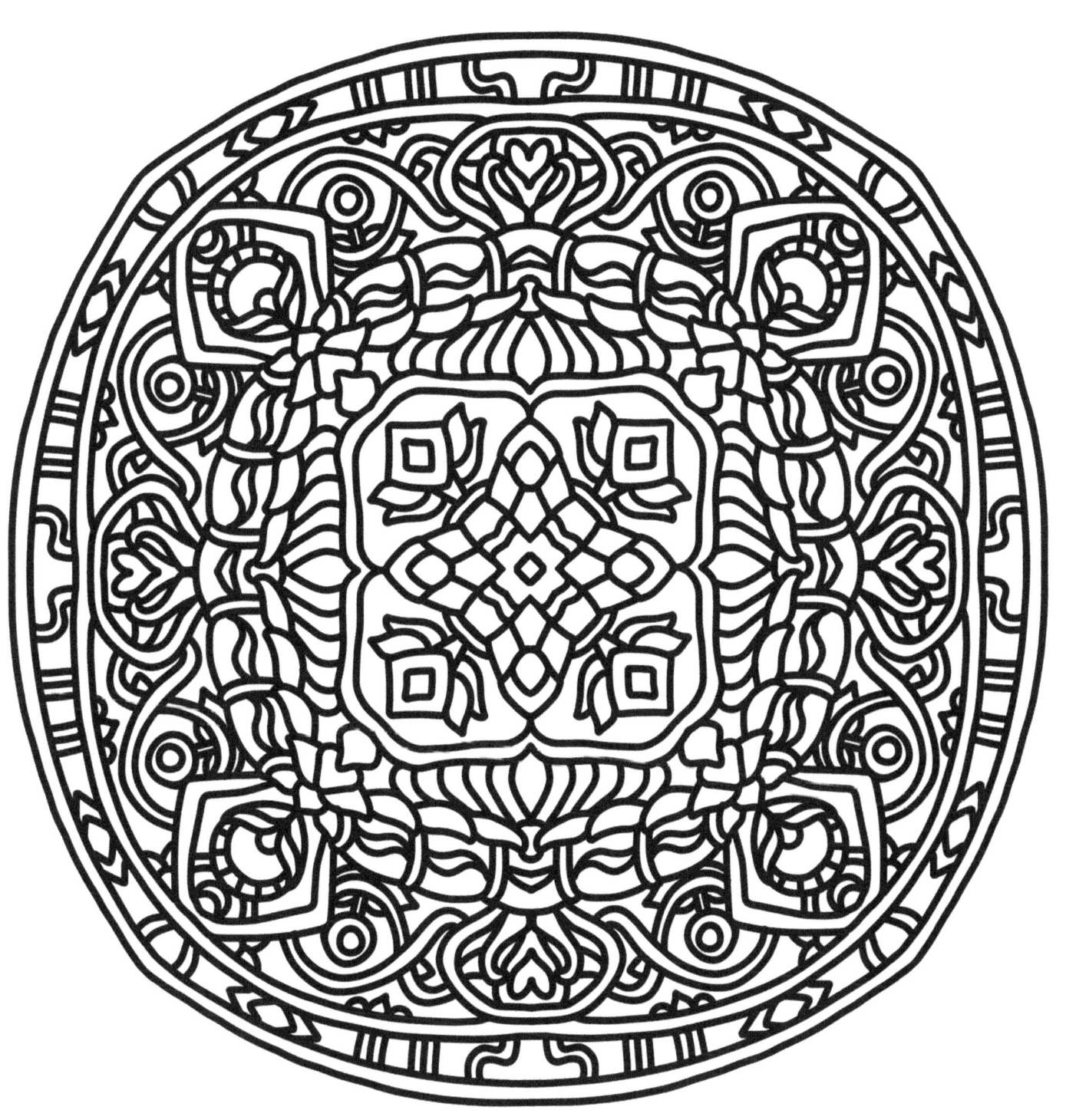

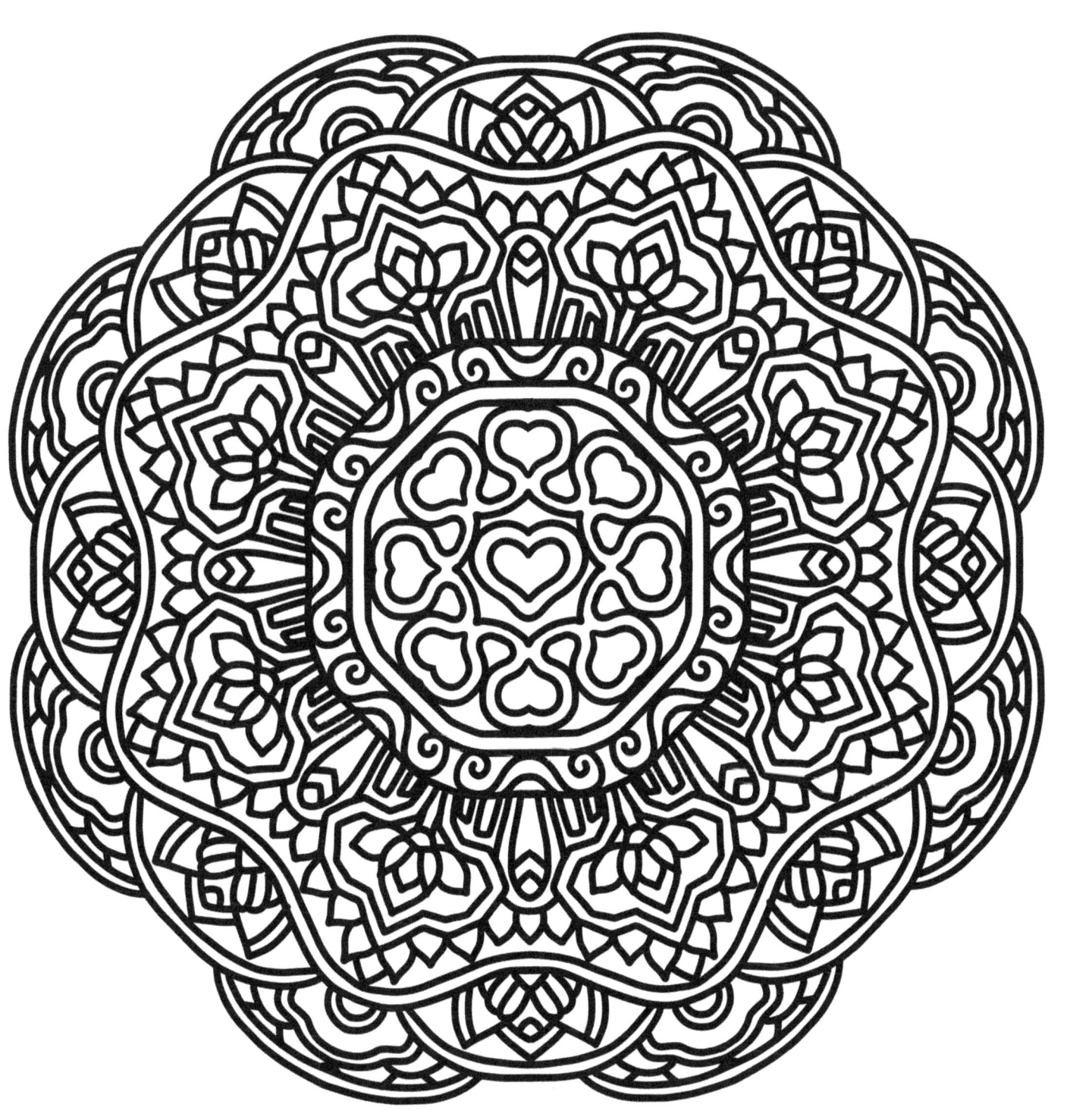

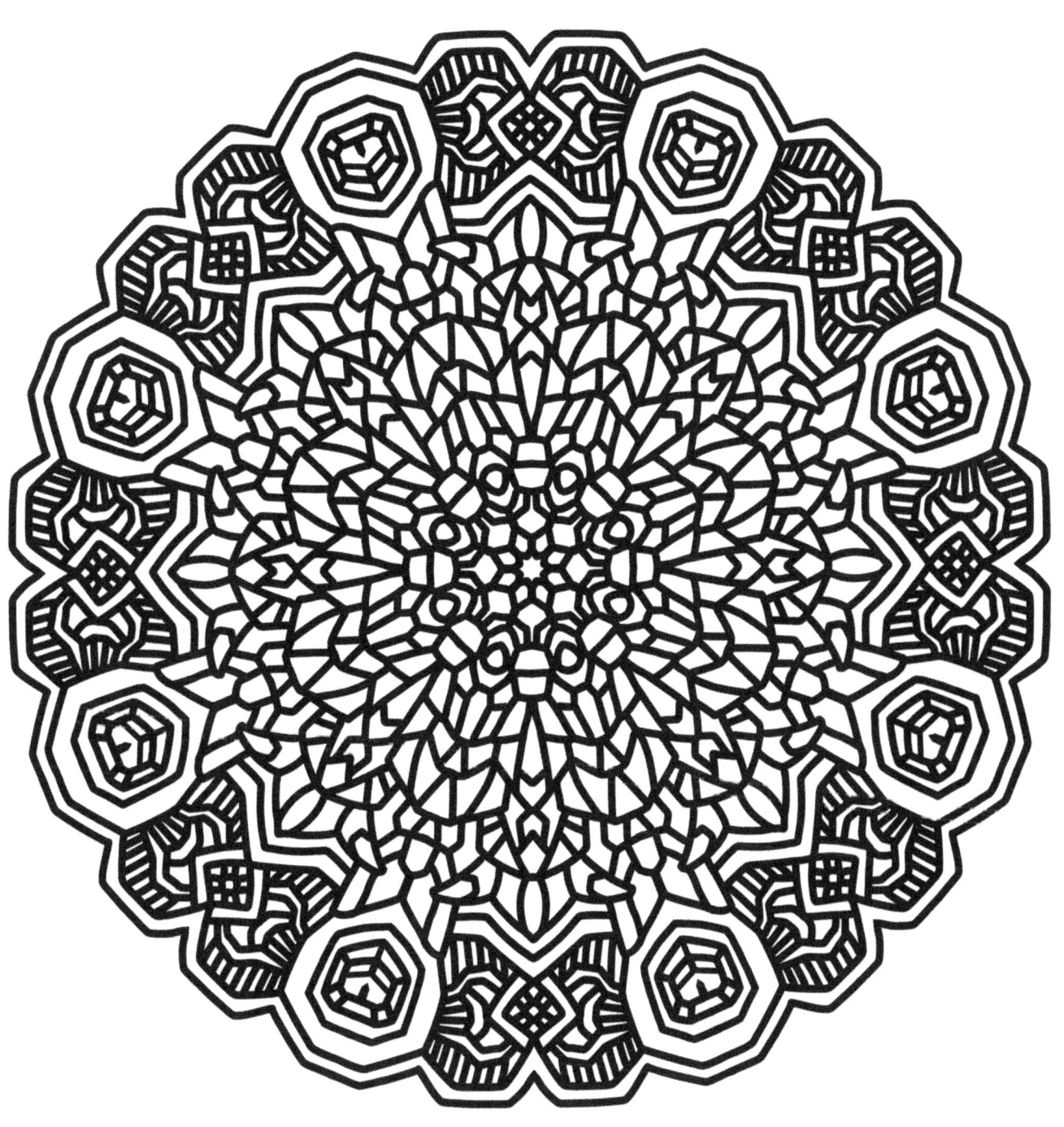

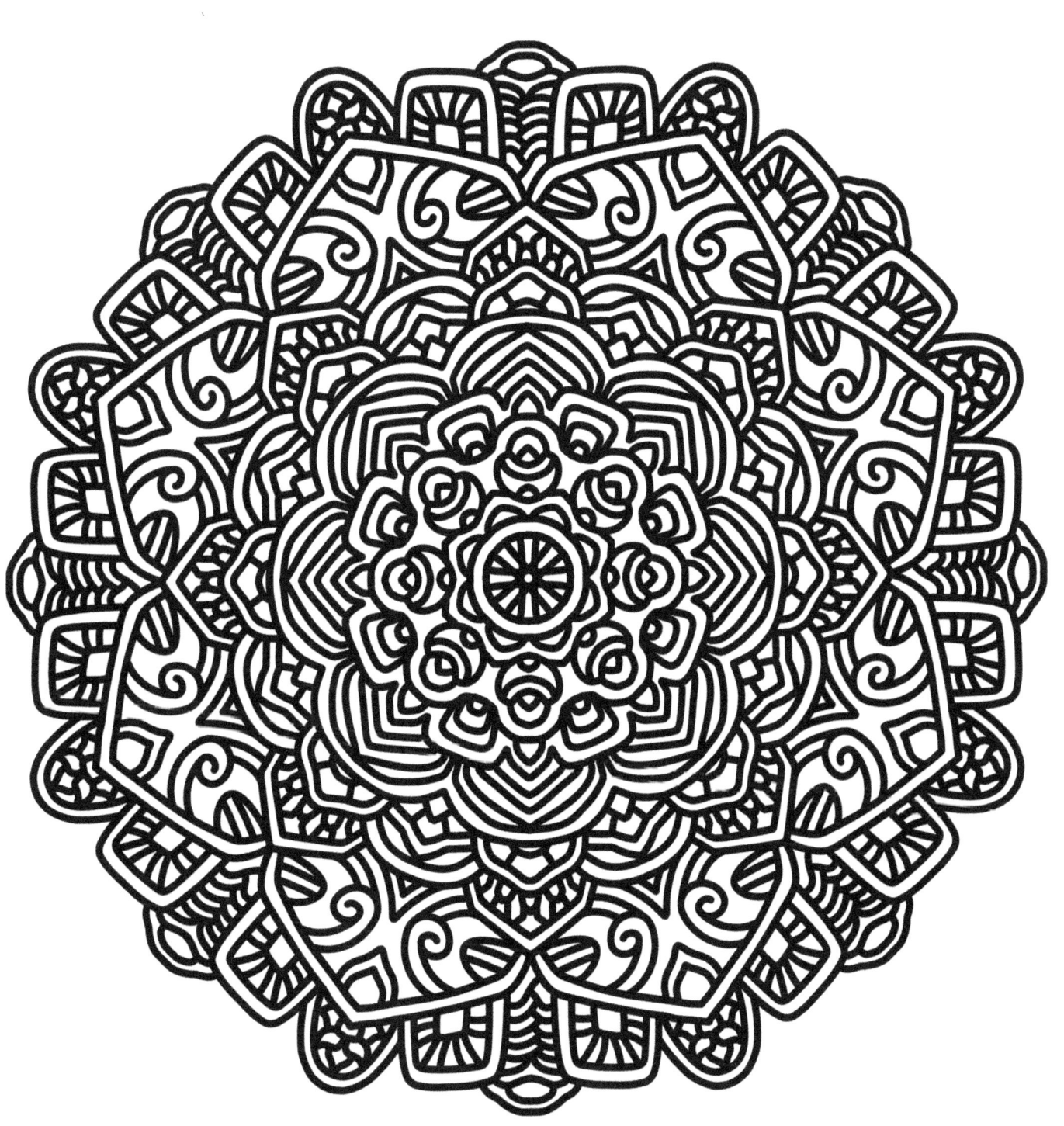

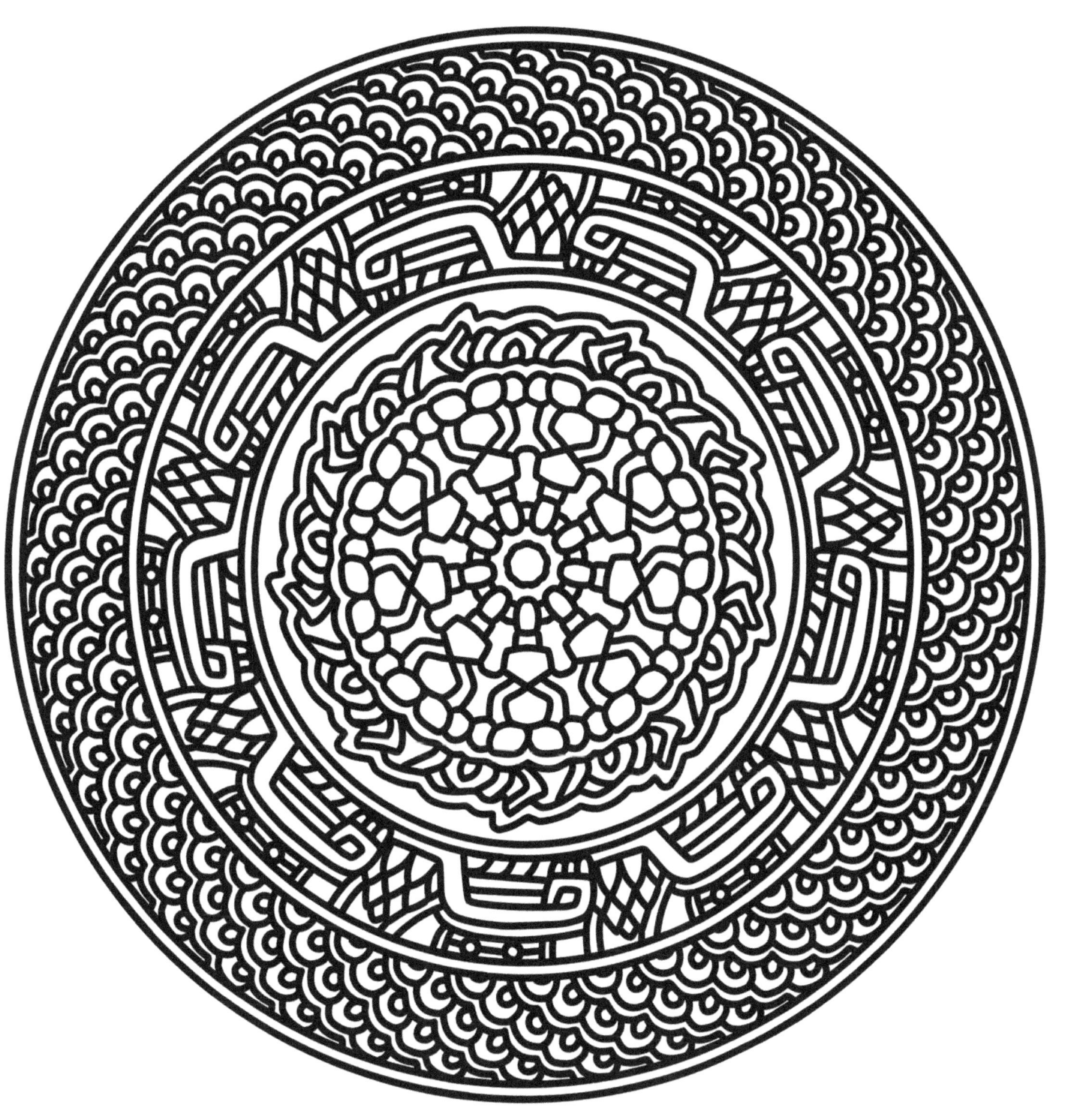

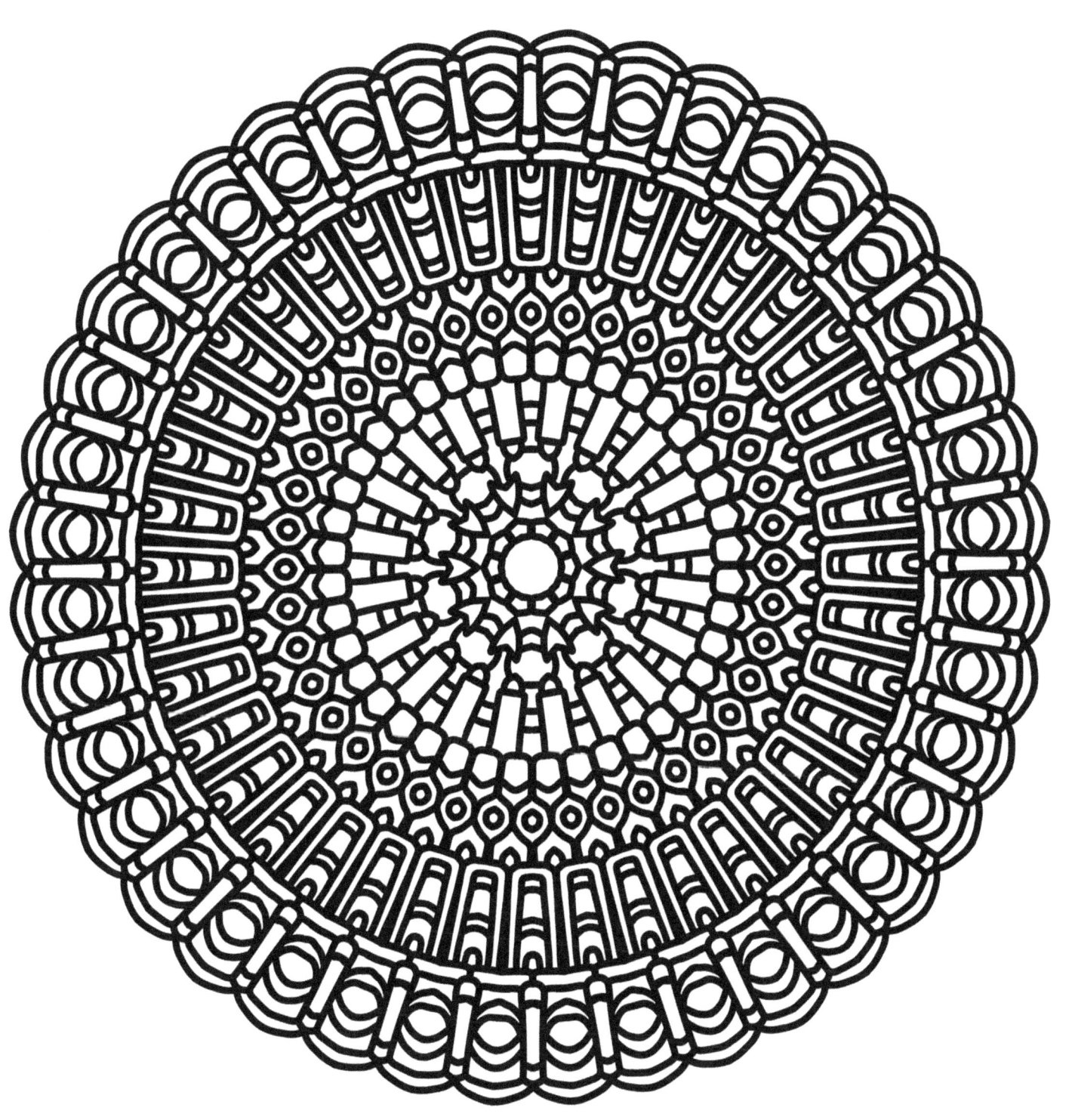

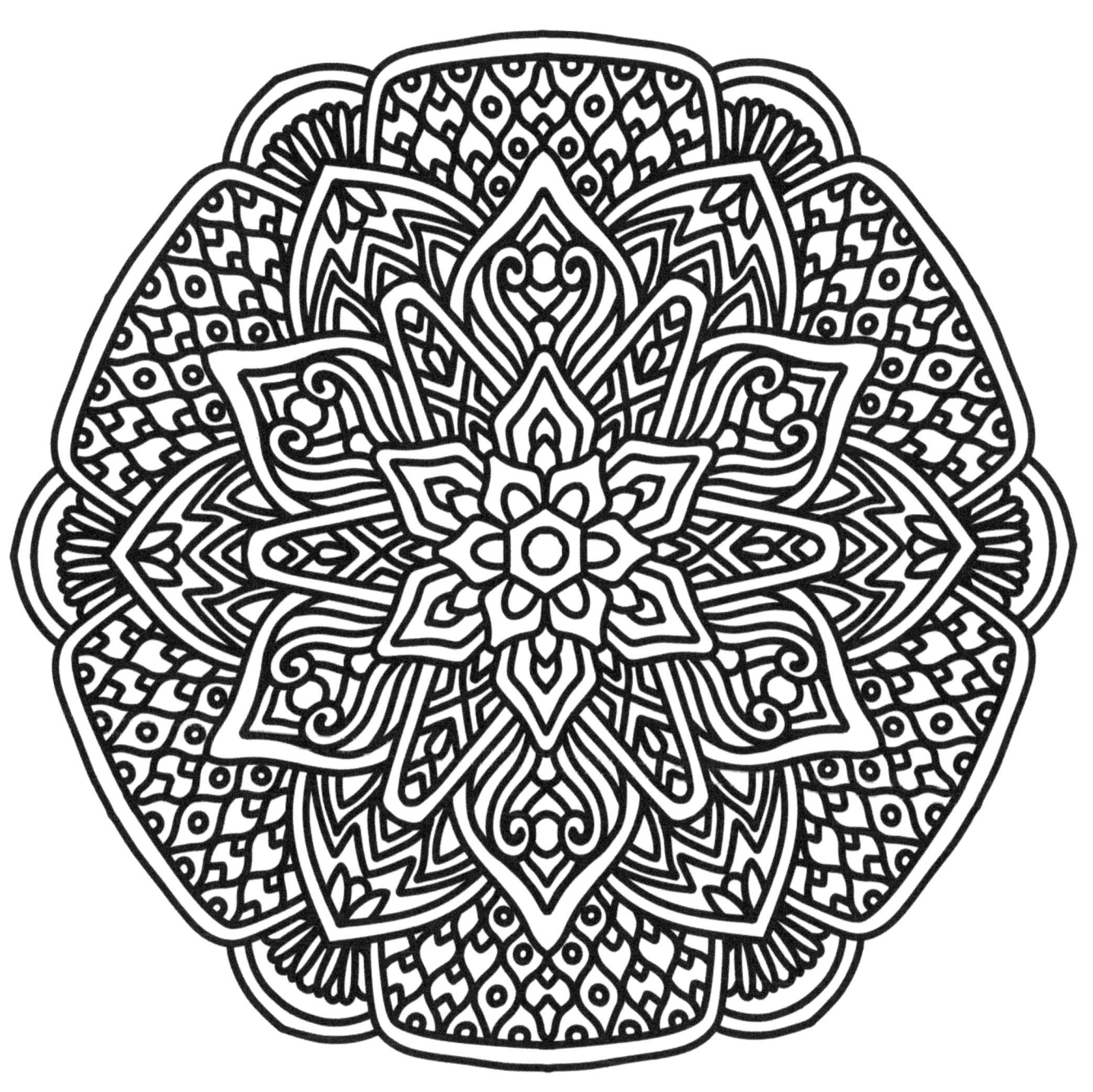

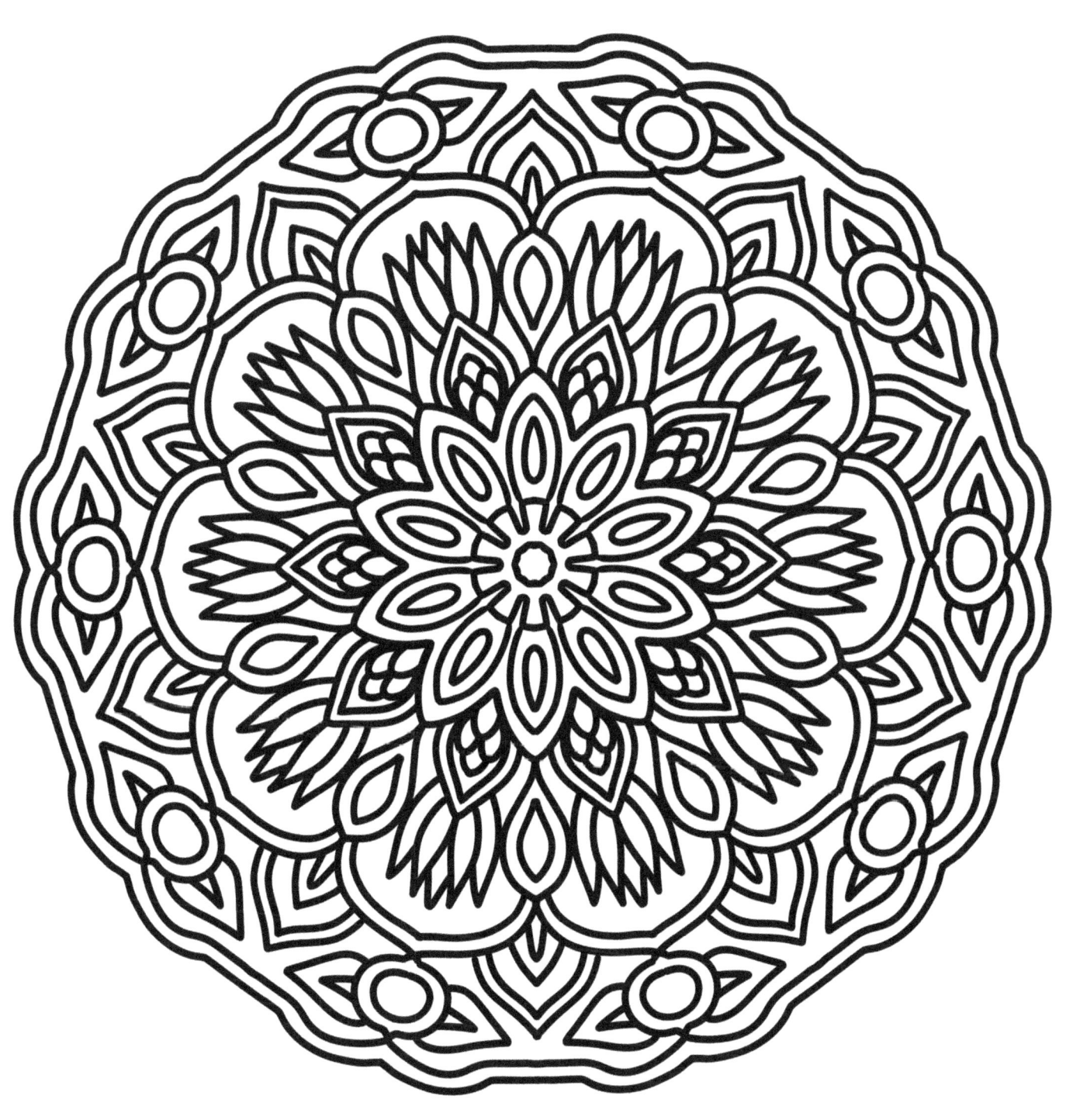

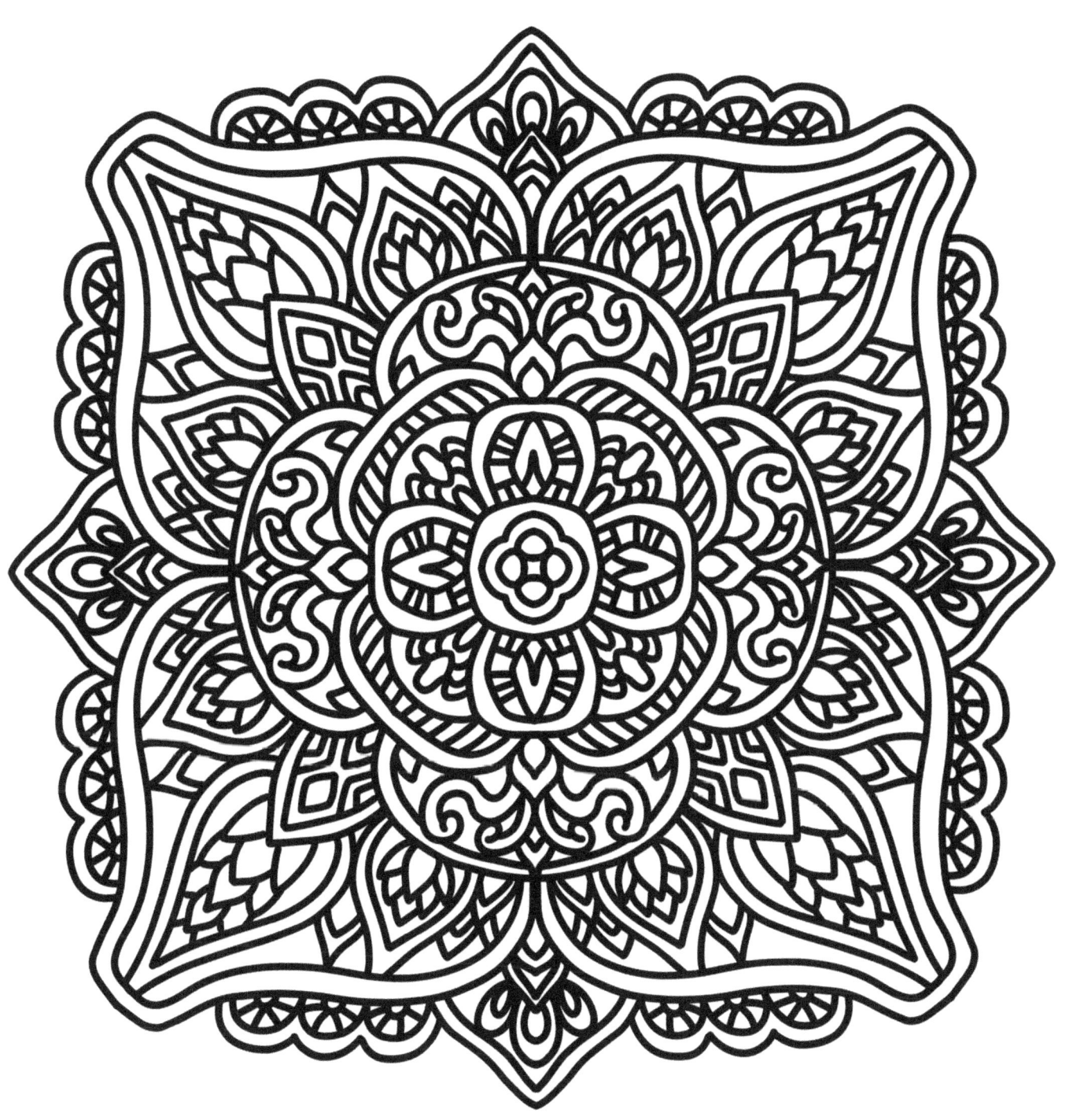

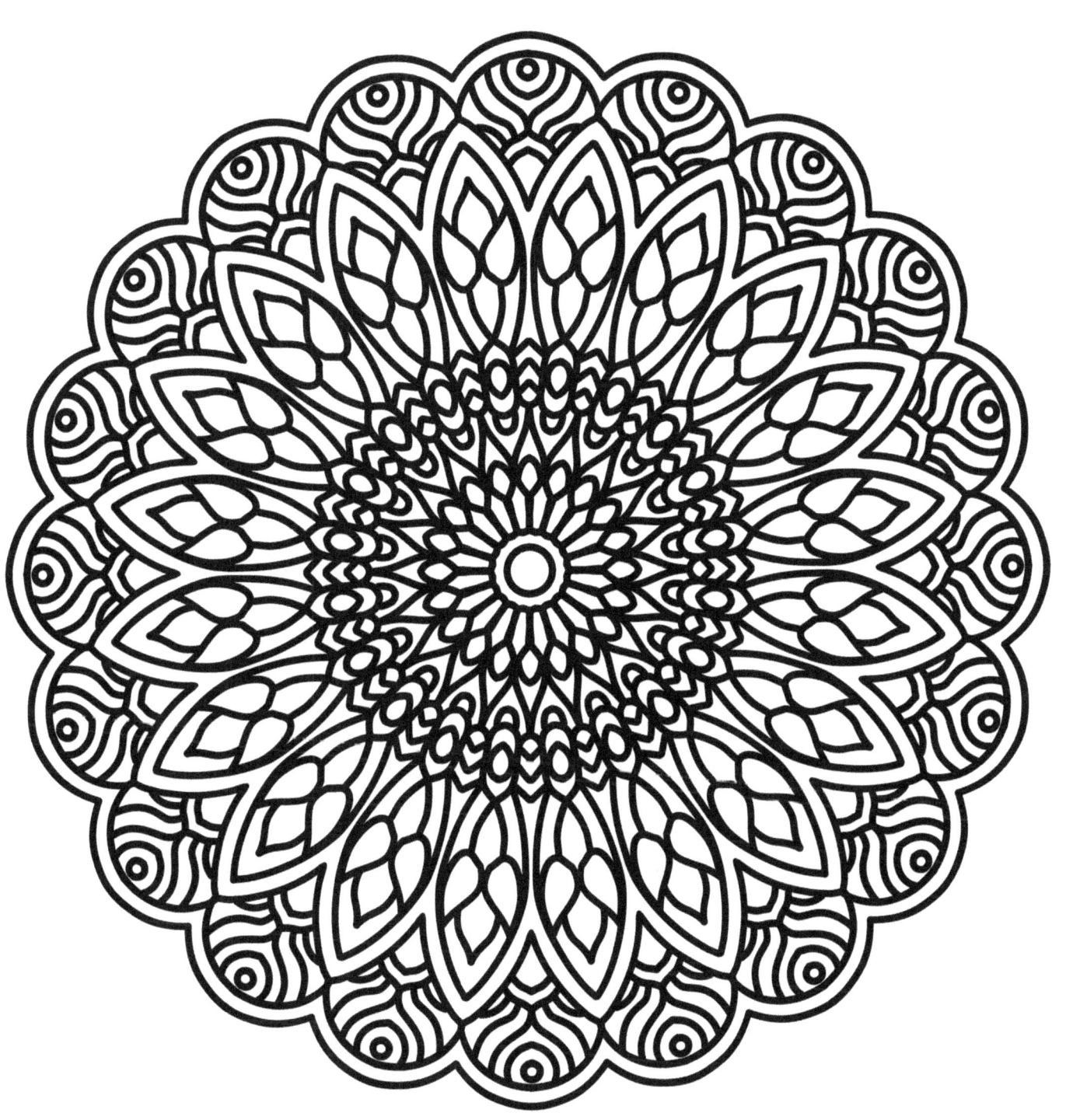

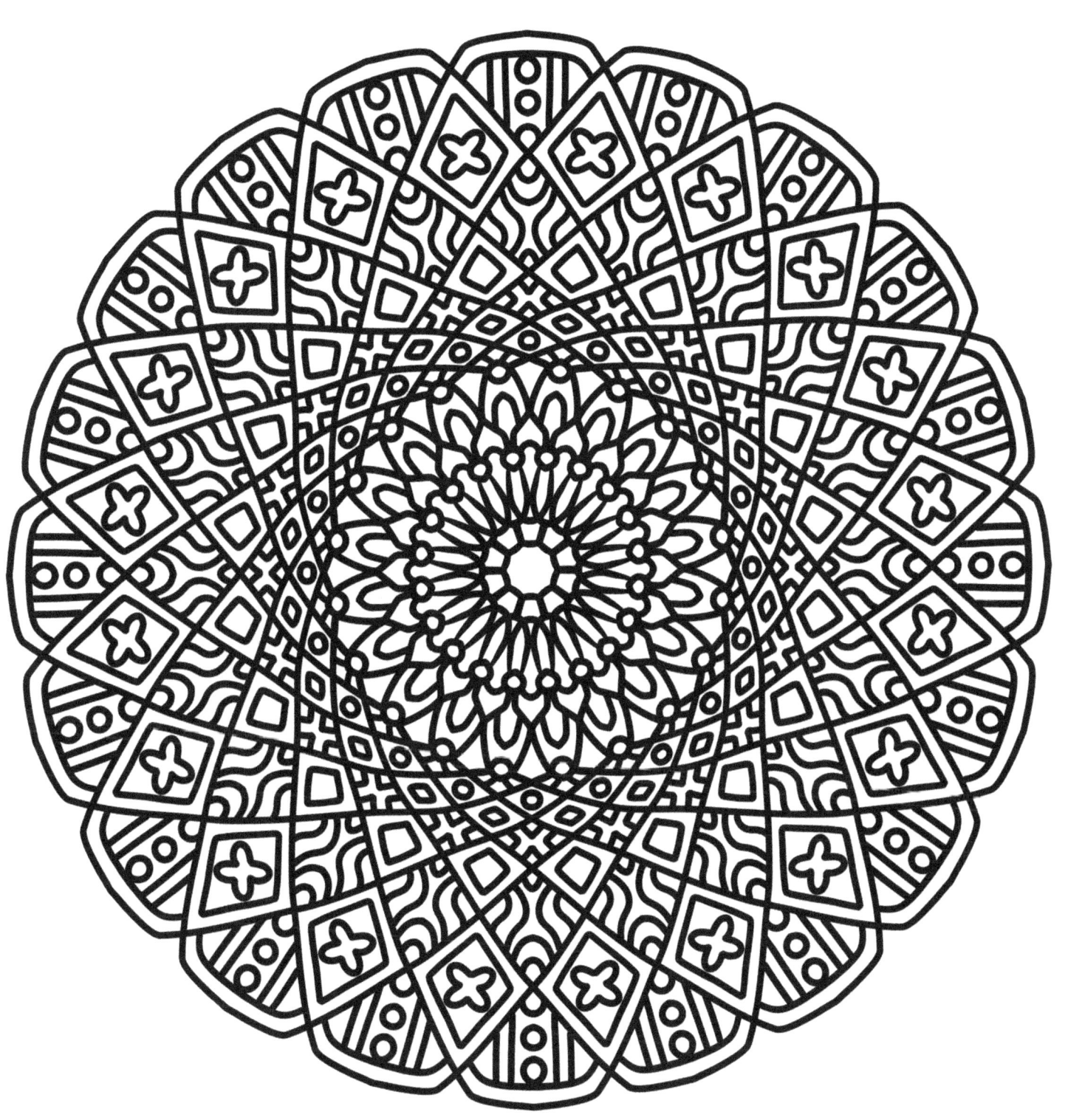

www.ingramcontent.com/pod-product-compliance
Lightning Source LLC
Chambersburg PA
CBHW080650180526
45168CB00008B/3365